Happy New Year!

by
SCHULZ

HarperHorizon

An Imprint of HarperCollins*Publishers*

Party Animals

Reflections
&
Resolutions

I THOUGHT I WAS THE LIFE OF THE PARTY WHEN I PUT THE LAMP SHADE ON MY HEAD..

THIS YEAR I HAVE RESOLVED NOT TO BE SO SERIOUS..I'M GOING TO TRY TO LAUGH MORE

I REMEMBER LAST YEAR YOU SAID YOU WERE GOING TO TRY TO BE A BETTER LISTENER..

HarperHorizon

An Imprint of HarperCollins Publishers

Produced by Jennifer Barry Design, Sausalito, CA
First published in 1998 by HarperCollins *Publishers* Inc.
http://www.harpercollins.com

ISBN 0-06-107301-6

Printed in Hong Kong

1 3 5 7 9 10 8 6 4 2